A HOME
IN PARIS

A HOME IN PARIS

INTERIORS · INSPIRATION

Photography by Guillaume de Laubier · Text by Catherine Synave

Flammarion

PAGE 2: The finely detailed facade of a seventeenth-century building on rue de Seine is decorated with classical masks and consoles supporting wrought-iron balconies.

FACING PAGE, FROM TOP LEFT: A Louis XV chest; an art-deco console; a charming gray marble mantelpiece; a statuette in Sèvres biscuit porcelain; a view of the Eiffel Tower from Montmartre; gilded *boiseries*; a 1960s Danish table with a Murano glass vase; an Egyptian Revival sphinx; a blond wood table, sheer cotton curtains, and paper lampshades— just a few of the decorative details to be discovered in Parisian homes.

PAGES 6–7: Viewed through the doorway, an intimate dining room is furnished with Austrian chairs dating from the 1860s and a table designed by Madeleine Castaing.

CONTENTS

INTRODUCTION

The buildings of Paris have an inimitable allure. Their facades create the distinctive Parisian cityscape; their stone takes on a golden hue as evening falls; their tall windows are fronted by lacy balconies; their slate roofs gleam a soft gray beneath the shifting sky. The apartments that lie behind those walls—some imposing, some quite modest—reveal a distinctively Parisian way of life. Some have retained their historic splendor, a testimony to the heritage of the stately world of the seventeenth and eighteenth centuries. Some are filled with treasures from the past, while others are the setting for contemporary designs. They may be showplaces for collections, furnishings, and decorative objects patiently amassed from the auction houses and galleries that abound in the city. Many designers live in neighborhoods traditionally frequented by artists and writers, and their apartments reflect a distinctive talent and savoir faire. Elsewhere, an unassuming doorway leads to a vast loft, a skillfully reconfigured space that conveys a taste for restraint and simplicity. Other dwellings are suffused with a sense of nostalgia, tranquil havens that recall times gone by.

TRADITION
AND
REINTERPRETATIONS

TRADITION,
PAST AND PRESENT

PAGE 12: In the vestibule of the Hôtel de Gesvres, a rendering of Madame de Pompadour in the guise of a sphinx reposes on the floor beside an eighteenth-century bust.

FACING PAGE, CLOCKWISE FROM TOP LEFT:
Boiseries designed by Directoire architects Percier and Fontaine flank an Empire faience stove and two portraits by Kucharsky.

Mounted next to a sunburst mirror, the silver Louis XIV sconce has a classical head in relief and arms decorated with acanthus leaves.

The salon features Empire-style doors; armchairs painted with flowers in the style of Empress Eugénie from the collection of Paul-Louis Weiller; a table by Lelièvre; and paintings by Alma Tadema.

The entrance hall is decorated with a plaster-cast statue and medallions made in the workshops of the Musées Nationaux.

Many distinguished buildings were constructed in Paris between the reigns of Louis XIV in the seventeenth century and Napoleon III in the mid-nineteenth. The fortunate residents who live in them today enjoy surroundings that are without peer—expressions of a refined taste that is universally admired. Some architectural details, damaged by the passage of time, have been restored. Designers have consulted archival records and studied period paintings and engravings to understand stylistic nuances. The rooms are laid out as an enfilade, with double doors opening directly from the reception rooms to the dining room and on to the bedrooms. This arrangement offers a free flow of movement from one space to the next, giving a dramatic sense of perspective. The floors may be of fine wood in *point de Versailles* parquet or chevron patterns; stone or marble tiles are sometimes inlaid with contrasting accents. The eye is drawn to ceiling cornices whose sculpted reliefs are covered with gold leaf. The *boiseries* and moldings reflect changing tastes, featuring plant and floral motifs, and sometimes insignias and masks.

The colors selected for walls and fabrics, crafted with incomparable expertise to preserve tradition, vary to harmonize with the furnishings. They may be intense, as in the seventeenth century, or lighter as preferred during the rococo era; cooler tones prevailed in the neoclassical style. Well-worn family pieces stand side by side with treasures discovered in the antique shops and auction houses of Paris. To add the finishing touches to the decor, paintings, sculptures, and drawings are displayed alongside carefully selected objets d'art.

Against backdrops that evoke the peerless French art of living, some designers choose to combine various genres. They upend conventional expectations, introducing touches of modernity without eradicating the formality of the past. Attuned to the elegance of a space, they construct a setting inspired by tradition, giving historical details fresh significance. The interior becomes a theater for staging twenty-first-century style, and showcasing groundbreaking contemporary design. An unexpected material may be hung on the wall, a stainless-steel chair may be placed in front of a gilded molding, a Mazarin desk next to a modernist table. Articles seem to shift almost at random from one room to another. The interior embraces these contrasts, and old and new coexist in a finely nuanced contradiction.

RUE DE RIVOLI

Only the original doors and dining room survive in this Empire-era apartment. The challenge for designer Jacques Garcia lay in recovering the original spirit of the place. He recreated the *boiseries* and elaborate parquet floors, evoking the life of the period by selecting furnishings and articles that all had their own history.

LEFT: Tadzio, named after the character in Visconti's film *Death in Venice*, assumes a pose on an Empire sofa originally used in the Grand Cabinet of the Château de Fontainebleau; the vertical stripes of color in a painting by Swiss visual artist John Armleder contrast with the muted swirls of gray in the painted faux marble walls.

FACING PAGE: The vestibule, inspired by Percier and Fontaine, the architects of rue de Rivoli, exemplifies the Empire taste for classical design and Greco-Roman statuary. The Ionic capitals of the columns and the coffers of the vaulted ceiling are an ideal setting for vases, finely worked urns, and a statue of Athena from the fourth century BCE. The chairs, bearing the stamp of the famed furniture maker Georges Jacob, were in the collections of the Château de Fontainebleau before being moved to the Tuileries.

RIGHT: The doors opening onto the enfilade at the entrance to the living room have been restored to their original colors based on samples from the period. The reliefs, moldings, and cornices have been decorated with gold leaf as they were in the nineteenth century. The vestibule can be glimpsed behind the sculpted head of a Celtic warrior set on a marble column.

BELOW: Designed by Percier and Fontaine, the dining room, with its infinitely reflecting mirrors, retains the wall coverings and decorative borders woven in Lyon in the nineteenth century. The room also boasts original *trumeaux* ornamented with Egyptian Revival vases and griffons with palmette reliefs.

LEFT: The living room leads to the library, where Jacques Garcia has placed an armchair bearing the stamp of the famed chair maker Jean-Baptiste Séné. Turgot, the Controller-General of Finance at the beginning of Louis XVI's reign, used this piece in his office.

BELOW, LEFT: The windows overlook the Tuileries Gardens. In the corner of the dining room stands a plaster cast of Antinous, Emperor Hadrian's favorite slave. The Musée Impérial commissioned this copy of the classical original.

BELOW, RIGHT: An antechamber furnished with chairs showing the patina of time. They have been re-covered with nineteenth-century velvet and repainted with foliate and floral motifs.

PAGES 20–21: The furnishings of the living room, which opens onto the dining room, have historic associations that make them treasured possessions. The armchairs with lion heads were court pieces, originally in Fontainebleau and later in the Tuileries; the mahogany table was in the Emperor Napoleon's council chamber in the Élysée Palace; the Louis XVI fire screen was among the furnishings owned by the Count of Artois, the king's brother.

IN SAINT-GERMAIN-DES-PRÉS

This three-level Directoire apartment was made larger through the purchase of an artist's studio on the bedroom level. Its owner—an aesthete who relishes mingling the traditional and the modern—took delight in blending these styles, with the assistance of decorator Tino Zervudachi.

LEFT: The walls of this traditional late eighteenth-century salon on the main floor are painted white with gray accents highlighting architectural details. The forms and materials of the room's furnishings and decorative objects create a harmonious blend of past and present: a "Oiseau" table by the Lalannes; a bergère by contemporary designer Tino Zervudachi; an armchair with Georges Jacob's distinctive stamp; Antony Gormley's linear metallic sculpture on the mantel; and the base of an eighteenth-century mahogany table.

ABOVE: In the same room, Daniel Chadwick's lighting fixture is reminiscent of Calder's mobiles. It seems to float weightlessly near a photograph of the moon originally taken by NASA and reinterpreted by Michael Light. The picture hangs above a Charles X officer's bed.

ABOVE, LEFT: A gilt bronze lamp is set like a sculpture on a polished steel seven-drawer chest (*semainier*) with decorative copper drawer pulls; the optical effect of a photograph featuring minuscule light bulbs echoes the image of the moon.

ABOVE, RIGHT: In the ground-floor entrance hall-cum-dining room, visitors are greeted by the upright figure of a rabbit sculpted in plaster by Andrea Branzi and a nineteenth-century bronze copy of a doe from Pompeii; Anselm Kiefer's *Jacob's Ladder* hangs on the wall.

LEFT: Accessible from the hall, the ground-floor living room is a resolutely contemporary space within a Directoire architectural setting. Nineteenth-century armchairs have been rejuvenated by white piqué upholstery. A painting by French-born American artist Arman, an accumulation of emphatic brushstrokes, announces the color scheme.

RIGHT: In a skillfully arranged juxtaposition, a bronze sculpture by Luiza Miller rears above a seventeenth-century Mazarin desk, and a Plexiglas table by McCollin Bryan harmonizes quite naturally with an eighteenth-century chair.

BELOW: On the third floor, a repurposed studio extends the bedroom and office into a master bathroom that is divided from the rest of the space by a simple arch. Here, tones of brown succeed the grays of the living rooms below. In deliberate contrast, the emerald green upholstery of the nineteenth-century English chairs emphasizes the subtlety of the master suite's tonalities.

ALONG THE GRANDS BOULEVARDS

Located in a building dating from 1795, Andrew Gn's apartment features a typical eighteenth-century layout. There is no connecting corridor; each room opens onto the next in an enfilade. The furniture, fabrics, and decorative objects tell the tale of the worldwide travels of this couturier, who was born in Singapore and has made London and Paris his adopted homes.

LEFT: An open door from the entrance hall gives a glimpse of the adjacent porcelain display room, filled with delicate pieces dating from the seventeenth and eighteenth centuries. Their pure blue and white tonalities stand out against the Chinese red walls and the gilded baroque consoles.

FACING PAGE: The smoking room beyond the porcelain room is furnished with tufted armchairs, a round table covered with embroidered velvet, Romantic-era portraits, and biscuit porcelain medallions. The setting evokes the mood of a nineteenth-century salon as described in a novel of the period.

PAGES 28–29: The bedroom's boudoir alcove is inspired by the British taste typified by Oscar Wilde. The walls are hung with old silks and brocades. The flowered silk used for the curtains is Andrew's own design. The Chinese porcelain and ceramics evoke the intermingling of cultures and styles that characterized the late nineteenth century.

RIGHT: To harmonize with the furniture styles, the rooms are painted in a variety of colors. The dining room, accessible from the entrance hall or the living room, has grayish walls in keeping with its eighteenth-century Swedish furnishings and the pink gown in the portrait of Lady Burlington. Her godmother was Empress Maria Theresa, the mother of Queen Marie-Antoinette.

BELOW, LEFT: The living room, which opens onto the bedroom and dining room, is painted a vibrant green drawn from the tone-on-tone brocade of the folding screens. It enhances the rich effect of the furnishings, which recall the splendor of a princely apartment. The room is an ideal setting for the gilt wood Regency console and the Louis XV armchairs.

BELOW, RIGHT: On a table in the smoking room, a Wedgwood vase and obelisk are displayed with a late nineteenth-century oil lamp to compose a charming still life.

RIGHT: Beneath a watercolor of a Swedish interior, an eighteenth-century Wedgwood basalt head of Mercury is posed on top of a china chest.

BELOW: In the dining room, a Louis XVI mirror hangs above a Provençal chest with the soft patina of age. It reflects an eighteenth-century German cartel clock and a seventeenth-century bust of Cleopatra in white Nevers faience. The kitchen is glimpsed beyond the door, which has been left just slightly ajar.

IN THE 7TH ARRONDISSEMENT

Retaining the original layout of the rooms, the decorator
and art dealer Klavs Rosenfalck restored the historic details of
a distinguished apartment situated on the main floor of a building
that dates from the time of Napoleon III. He furnished it with
designs from the 1950s and 1960s to give the home new roots in
the twentieth century.

LEFT: Playing with contrasting effects
and enlivening the setting, the office's
walls are covered with aluminum
leaf. A striking monumentally scaled
painting by Anne-Marie Pécheur is
simply tilted against the wall.

FACING PAGE: The entrance hall
doors are fine examples of highly
skilled restoration work. On the
door opening to the living room, the
frames and reliefs have recovered
their original elegance, and the
moldings have been carefully re-
gilded. A contemporary Italian steel
and glass chair and a vintage floor
lamp seem to flaunt their contrasting
aesthetic sensibilities.

FACING PAGE: At one end of the dining room, a gold vinyl ottoman, a silky smooth sofa, and a custom-designed carpet seem at ease in the exquisitely detailed setting with its gilded *boiseries.*

LEFT: The ceiling height made it possible to build a guest room on the mezzanine level, the only space with a distinctively contemporary feel. Simple steps made from oak and suspended from ropes lead up to a dressing room located behind a glass balustrade.

BELOW: The living room is a tribute to the splendors of the past. Modern designer furniture and decorative objects comfortably adapt to a backdrop of gilt *boiseries.* Vast mirrors, reflecting the light, further expand the space.

PAGES 36–37: In the office—accessible through the living room or the bedroom—the gray of the *boiseries*, juxtaposed with the aluminum wall covering, has a calming effect. The spare design of the 1960s Danish furniture, signed by Fabricius & Kastholm, fits perfectly with the decor.

RIGHT: With its custom-made furniture, stove hood, and lacquered cupboard, the kitchen offers a striking contrast of gray and vivid orangey-red.

BELOW, LEFT: The only brightly colored note on the walls of the apartment reflects Italian taste. The walls and reliefs in the bedroom, which opens onto the office, are painted a shade of red that magnifies the impact of a photographic portrait of Marilyn Monroe.

BELOW, RIGHT: The lacquered doors of the kitchen cabinets reflect a room that is furnished with wooden components protected by stainless-steel surfaces.

FACING PAGE: In the dining room, the richly decorated ceiling, cornices, moldings, *trumeaux*, *boiseries*, and gilding glimmer in two vast, infinitely reflecting mirrors. The decor of Napoleon III's era is a superlative showcase for contemporary designer furniture and lighting.

A STONE'S THROW FROM
THE TUILERIES GARDENS

The fashion designer Alexis Mabille left his apartment's rooms as they were during the Directoire era, in a classic enfilade. The look is enlivened with a touch of whimsy, and candles alone provide the light for the furnishings and objects, creating a theatrical setting.

LEFT: In the living room, books on art and fashion, sources of inspiration, overflow the bookshelves and are stacked on a bookcase flanked by Gothic Revival columns by Viollet-le-Duc. Mirrors, placed at random on the mantel, facing simple cubic coffee tables, or leaning against a wall, reflect the room in fragmented and unexpected images. A tapestry by Laurence Dervaux, with a distinctively 1940s design, covers a Louis-Philippe banquette.

ABOVE: Piano lamps cast a soft light over library shelves where a few selected pieces are arranged in a nostalgic composition: a butterfly and a portrait of Alexis Mabille by Tina Barney are displayed beneath a pale pink parrot and boxes for detachable collars.

PAGES 42–43: In the dining room, a spirit of illusionism and incongruity prevails. A console composed of various decorative elements takes the place of a mantelpiece. Mirrors from the 1940s and Napoleon III's era are interlopers within the gilt frame. Chairs from an Egyptian palace stand near an ebony tabletop set on trestles, whose legs seem to jostle each other.

RIGHT: A still life is created from a silver Louis XIV sconce, mercurized and silver-plated candleholders, and bronze torches. In the evening, a host of white tapers illuminates the apartment, and mirrors reflect their flickering light into infinite space.

BELOW: An eighteenth-century gilt wood screen stands in a corner of the dining room by the door to the entry hall. It has retained the original jute covering applied before the panels were covered with silk or brocade. Its simplicity harmonizes with the sculptor's modeling stand and the spare lines of the Napoleonic army folding chairs.

FACING PAGE: The Napoleon III bed in the bedroom was restored and upholstered with white fabric, giving it a contemporary look. Its sensibility harmonizes with the modernity of Suzanne Junker's photograph *Le Rhône et la Saône*, where a modern woman's face contrasts with classical sculpted masks.

ON THE CHAMPS-ÉLYSÉES

The Haussmann-era architecture of fashion designer
Alexandre Zouari's apartment lends itself to exuberant colors;
these are inspired by the work of Madeleine Castaing,
a legendary figure in the design world of the twentieth century.

LEFT: In the living room, English furniture mingles with Arman's "Danceuse" armchairs. The gilding of the Directoire mirror and the Oriental subjects of the paintings stand out against the cherry-red wall covering, which is bordered with colorful strips cut from a shawl. The rich tones are repeated in the sofa's upholstery.

ABOVE: On a richly ornamented bookshelf that could easily be pictured in a British colonial residence, two Indian figurines in full regalia are mounted on lamp bases flanking a Sèvres porcelain jardiniere.

PAGES 48–49: On either side of the dining room's doorway to the living room, two plaster consoles by Emilio Terry challenge decorative conventions. The tall eighteenth-century mirrors reflecting the room show a quintessential Parisian apartment designed for entertaining.

RIGHT: The bedroom is given a warm glow by the orange flannel wall covering that harmonizes with the wood tones of the Biedermeier secretary and the armchairs with ebony accents. Like the lamps and decorative objects, they are from Madeleine Castaing's residence.

BELOW: In the bedroom, colors interplay and shift with the changing light. The decorative details evoke the spirit of exotic travel: the headboard has a Middle Eastern form, the bench is covered with a kilim carpet, the rug has a leopard-skin pattern, the bedside tables are English and Austrian, and the watercolors depict the Roman forum.

LEFT: Enlivening the entrance and recalling the interiors of old Saint Petersburg, the Wedgwood-blue walls are ornamented with a frieze of stenciled motifs that accent the outlines of the doors and paneling.

BELOW, LEFT: A crystal chandelier illuminates the entry hall. Its doors open onto the surrounding rooms as if onto stage sets. One entrance reveals the vibrantly green hall leading to the living room. Hanging above a 1930s sideboard, a painting by Satch seems to be a natural fit.

BELOW, RIGHT: On the walls, chairs, and lampshades, in the living room and throughout the apartment, colors abound and complement each other. They bring the decorative ensemble to life.

NEAR THE PALAIS-ROYAL

In their search for a Parisian pied-à-terre, interior designers Joseph Achkar and Michel Charrière sought an apartment steeped in the history of the city. The Hôtel de Gesvres, built in the seventeenth century, was exactly what they were looking for. Their restoration has revived the building's former splendor and grace.

ABOVE: The vestibule, its floor paved with stone and slate, remains as it was when it served as the guardroom of the Duke of Gesvres, governor of the city of Paris. Studies of the inventory and archives have revealed how the residence was furnished, and give details of daily life there.

ABOVE, LEFT: Layers of paint had to be stripped away to restore the original colors of a Regency console: blue on a red base coat.

ABOVE, RIGHT: One of the adjoining salons in the imposing enfilade of rooms. A rare seventeenth-century cabinet of mirrors remains in situ in Paris, with an exceptional Louis XIV gilt wood daybed and a silver eighteenth-century English table.

RIGHT: The overdoor ornamentation flanked by winged griffons frames a portrait of Madame de Sévigné from the sale of the Château de Bercy.

PAGES 54–55: Accessed from the hall, the eighteenth-century salon with Louis XVI *boiseries* was formerly the footmen's antechamber. The furniture bears the signatures of the era's greatest cabinetmakers, including Séné, Riesener, and Jacob.

RIGHT: In the cabinet of mirrors used for entertaining dinner guests, metal decorative objects dating from the seventeenth century are arranged on a gilt wood Louis XIV console. It was executed based on a design by the seventeenth-century designer and engraver Jean Le Pautre.

BELOW, LEFT: A precious Mughal coffer fashioned from ivory and tortoiseshell rests on a Louis XV table signed by Meunier. It fits in gracefully with a Regency armchair that retains its original paint.

BELOW, RIGHT: The gilt bronze lock on a door leading to the entrance hall is decorated with winged griffons, similar to those in Versailles.

ABOVE, LEFT: Arrayed on the porphyry tabletop of a console decorated with angels in the style of painter Charles Lebrun, a seventeenth-century vermeil lion and a Yemenite alabaster urn lend an Oriental touch to the cabinet of mirrors.

ABOVE, RIGHT: The salon's eighteenth-century mantel is decorated with gilt bronzes by Pitoin. Boasting a royal heritage, an identical clock is displayed in the Trianon, and the table is from the Schloss Charlottenburg in Berlin.

RIGHT: The bedroom once occupied by the Duke of Gesvres is now one of the salons in the enfilade, decorated with seventeenth- and eighteenth-century pieces: an alabaster and marble bust, a fire screen with decoration by Bérain, a European lacquer table, and a sofa and armchairs with their original tapestry upholstery.

MODERN AND CONTEMPORARY INTERIORS

SPACE AND COLOR
FOR A FRESH APPROACH
TO THE PARISIAN ART OF LIVING

PAGE 58: A playful display of convex PVC mirrors, a stainless-steel lamp by Hubert Le Gall, and a painting by an Oceanic artist created with a single continuous stroke of paint.

FACING PAGE, CLOCKWISE FROM TOP LEFT
Reminiscent of a New York loft, a bicycle is propped beneath a traditional glass-paneled wall on one side of the kitchen.

A sofa upholstered with textured linen has satin cushions; the doorway is hung with panels of wool in various checkered patterns.

The armchair is by George Nelson.

An architect's table dating from the 1920s stands in front of a luminous mirror.

Whether they were formerly commercial premises—studios, warehouses, or garages—or simply conventional apartments, today's interiors reinvent the past. They express a sense of modernity, representing a fresh approach to the Parisian *art de vivre*. Exquisite lacquers and delicate silks are fearlessly juxtaposed with industrial staples, including raw and polished concrete and metal. A glass panel may serve as a dividing wall, facilitating construction on different levels. Sometimes the traditional concept of a single-purpose room is discarded: living room, dining room, and kitchen may occupy the same space, simplifying daily life.

Light plays an essential role in these remodeled structures. Lofty French windows open onto city or garden views; glass blocks arranged in geometric patterns may be used for windows or floors. The lighting is subtly modulated as evening falls, transforming the ambience of the space.

In some of these homes, color is used to enliven architecture dating from Haussmann's era, reconfiguring a wall or altering its appearance. A bold variety of shades appears in fabrics and furnishings that recall the decorating trends that have succeeded each other over recent decades. Elsewhere, color is used as a lively accent on a chair, sofa, curtain, rug, or wall, taking inspiration from the Bauhaus and cubism.

Furniture, painstakingly collected, bears the signatures of legendary cabinetmakers, whose iconic works are exhibited in design and decorative arts museums all over the world; they are tributes to the creativity and cultural wealth of the twentieth and twenty-first centuries. The lines are simple; right angles frequently replace curvilinear forms, and metal is often a prominent component. These furnishings blend discreetly with the architecture, creating a setting for sculpture, decorative objects, and photographs—all those personal acquisitions that make a house distinctive and capture the spirit of the moment.

IN MONTMARTRE

It started out as a concrete block—a parking garage where movie
director Jean-Jacques Beineix shot *Diva*. After five months
of renovation work, it became a custom-designed home where
the bedrooms, set on platforms, open onto the living area
and a bay window—the only natural source of light. Welcome
to the home of interior designer Tristan Auer.

LEFT: On one side of the living room, a windowed wall runs the length of the garden courtyard. On the other side, a polished concrete divider topped with glass panels separates this space from the bedrooms, which are both accessible and private. The walls are painted a timeless neutral tone. The furniture was designed by Tristan Auer, with the carpets and fabrics providing color. Simplicity is akin to serenity in this interior.

ABOVE: The living room is reached by passing through the kitchen, which is painted a sophisticated tone of gray and decorated with a nineteenth-century mirror to give this utilitarian space the air of a boudoir.

PAGES 64–65: Steps sculpted from solid oak lead to the raised platform that opens onto the bedrooms. The design of the library, the Guilloché enameled metal that backs the shelves, and the pure lines of Charlotte Perriand's table are all design choices that evoke the industrial heritage of the building before its transformation.

FACING PAGE: Simplicity is the keynote of a home where everything is readily accessible, working together to facilitate family life. None of the furniture is fragile; none of the objects is precious. A metal chair in the style of Jean Prouvé is paired with a 1940s desk.

LEFT: The bathroom located next to the bedroom faces over the street. Frosted glass "bottle base" inserts protect the room from prying eyes and provide kinetic lighting effects.

BELOW, LEFT: To separate the sofa from the platform and the glass wall, Tristan Auer created a sheltering surround with a screen fashioned from lacquer and Cordoba leather.

BELOW, RIGHT: Light plays a preeminent role here. In the evening, fifteen different light sources throughout the apartment illuminate the rooms, creating a distinctive mood.

IN SAINT-GERMAIN-DES-PRÉS

Antique dealer and interior architect Florence Lopez decided
to move into the neighborhood that she visited almost daily.
She was familiar with its every nook and cranny. She imbued
a 1920s studio with the Bauhaus spirit, changing the furniture
and wall colors annually, sweeping conceptual cobwebs away.

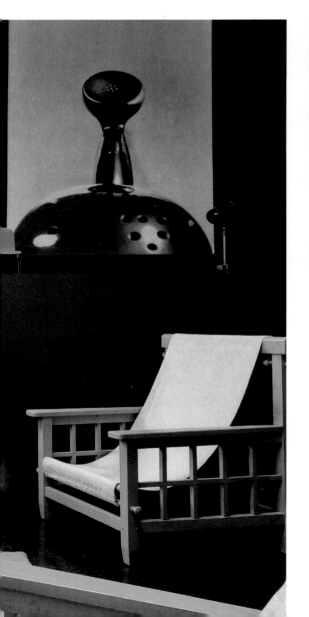

LEFT: On one side, an entryway opens onto the studio; on the other, the kitchen and two small bedrooms follow one after another. Each is painted a different color, forming a backdrop for furnishings and objects that represent her tireless quest to achieve an iconic interpretation of modernism. Florence Lopez's clients are on the right path when they climb the four steep flights of stairs to her aerie.

ABOVE: The door to the studio remains as it was originally, retaining its 1920s windowpanes, some of which are clouded with age. The matte black of the walls gives the impression of depth and timelessness. On the mantel, a photograph by Ruth Francken defies our established notions of the telephone.

ABOVE, LEFT: The Jean Royère sofa had to be dismantled to reveal his signature. The bright yellow awnings protect the immense south-facing windows.

ABOVE, RIGHT: The kitchen features Bauhaus gray and primary colors, evoking a constructivist painting. It is suffused with the aesthetic of Theo Van Doesburg, the Dutch founder of the de Stijl movement; the tabletop and lighting fixture near a painting by Edward Steinberg echo each other's perfectly circular forms.

LEFT: Florence Lopez happened on the studio by chance one snowy day some twenty years ago. She was captivated by its sense of incongruity and has never tired of its view over the roofs of eighteenth-century buildings and the sky. She promptly settled into a studio space that is ideal for the creation of her distinctive interiors.

RIGHT: Three colors—orange, black, and blue—dominate the bedroom, which is accessed through the kitchen. To create the impression of paneling, two of the walls are painted in different tones.

BELOW, LEFT: Placed near the window, this Marcel Breuer chaise longue is one of his very first models. Made from laminated wood, lacquered as it was originally, it is a rare specimen.

BELOW, RIGHT: An American piece made of eight lacquer and walnut boxes featuring blond tonalities is used as a chest. A few treasured articles are arranged around a steel lamp by an unknown designer that dates from the 1940s.

RUE SAINTE-ANNE

In an old Parisian neighborhood where most textile producers are located, Bianca and Vincent Frey renovated the structure that had been the warehouse of Pierre Frey, the eponymous fabric designer, in the 1950s. His grandson Vincent carries on the business today. He took advantage of the interplay of spaces, retaining the original ceilings and floors as far as possible.

ABOVE: The entrance door opens onto a spacious area beneath the mezzanine. The living room's carpet design is based on a motif found in archives dating to the 1950s. The fabrics from Pierre Frey's collections were selected based on a love of color and a determination to prove that a loft's palette need not be limited to white and gray.

ABOVE, LEFT: "La Paix," a Clara Halter design produced by Frey, is printed on a glass panel in the kitchen, which is located beneath the mezzanine.

ABOVE, RIGHT: To allow the flood of light from the lofty glass wall to suffuse the building, the architect recessed the mezzanine level, freeing up space for the dining room. The ground floor's height makes a spectacular impression. Glass pavements from the 1930s are used for the floor.

RIGHT: The kitchen wall serves as an art gallery, featuring an anodized aluminum sculpture by Victoria Wilmotte. The wooden flooring is original—oak mellowed by the patina of age.

PAGES 74–75: The mezzanine housing the parents' and children's bedrooms features three 1970s hanging lamps suspended at different heights. Through the skylight, they provide illumination for the kitchen below.

RIGHT: The pastel, silky blue of the bamboo fiber carpeting, paired with a velvet pillow and soft cotton throw, lends an aura of serenity to the bedroom.

BELOW: There are no superfluous details in the master bedroom, which is separated from the adjacent bathroom by a freestanding wall panel. The ethereal lightness of the "Illusion" wallpaper and the subtle mystery of Joakim Eneroth's photograph *Alone With Others* make the space an ideal refuge.

TOP, LEFT: A flight of steps descends to a corridor leading to the kitchen. The pure lines of the staircase contrast with the bulky form of the vintage table-football game, a popular focus at the weekend.

BOTTOM, LEFT: In a windowless bathroom, a "Mauritius" print linen curtain evokes the colors of a tropical forest. The water in the shower pours down like soft summer rain. The rounded forms of Eero Saarinen's "Tulip" chair for Knoll harmonize with the setting.

BELOW: The children's room seen from the mezzanine. The ground-floor entrance is visible at the foot of the stairs.

BY THE CHAMP-DE-MARS

Color is at the heart of Mary Shaw's life, as well as her designs. She displays its infinite variations from one room to the next in her apartment. Flouting the Parisian conventions of Haussmannian subdued stone and slate tonalities, she confronts us with surprising harmonies.

LEFT: The china cabinet in the kitchen brims with Celtic-inspired stoneware plates and cups, whose simplicity appeals to contemporary sensibilities. Like the fabrics, furnishings, and accessories, they are produced by Sequana, the design collaborative founded by Mary Shaw.

FACING PAGE: As is frequently the case in nineteenth-century buildings, the entrance hall gives access onto the living room and bedrooms. Choosing a vivid green that reminds her of Irish meadows, Mary reveals her distinctive taste and her love of nature. The bronze and cast-iron coat rack takes the form of a tree, and a hanging painted with Virginia creeper brings the garden inside. A crown of dry leaves serves as a lampshade. Deep red and plum-colored hangings form a backdrop in the cloakroom.

PAGES 80–81: In the salon, daringly painted vermilion walls highlight the details of the paneling. The background color enhances the range of saturated purple and violet tonalities in the linen satin and leather upholstery.

LEFT: A glass-paneled door separates the red living room from the adjacent space with its ocher walls. A black table with elegant lines is set for tea. In the windows, tartan panels harmonize with a Virginia creeper motif.

BELOW, LEFT: Evocative of a country setting, a fire glows in the hearth of the ocher living room. Colors and materials mingle and complement each other: the tones of the walls, the soft rose of a vintage cashmere shawl, the purple tweed upholstery of an English armchair, and the vivid green of the leather covering an oak bench.

BELOW, RIGHT: Mary is intrigued by Romanesque and Gothic art, which suggests a kind of minimalism to her. She took inspiration from the paved flooring of the church in Saint-Benoît-sur-Loire to design this tabletop of enameled glass, which never leaves its place of honor here.

LEFT: Once again, there is harmony between the green of the entrance and the yellow of the kitchen glimpsed through the open door. Visitors move serenely from one room to the next.

BELOW: The bedroom features a subtle interplay among the pastels of fine woolens and satin-weave linens. The only vivid accent is a red lampshade. The curtain and overlaid voile panel covering the window filter the light, creating the impression of shifting shadows.

PLAINE MONCEAU

The house belonging to architect and designer Charles Zana, set in an urban garden, dates back to 1870. The rooms of this three-story dwelling demonstrate an Italian design sensibility characterized by humor and whimsical invention.

LEFT: On the second floor, an oak bookshelf forms a display case for books and objects, enclosing the space in which sofas are also placed at right angles. A neon standing lamp by Ettore Sottsass embodies the precepts of Studio Alchimia, the first design movement to use laminates in the 1970s. Two collector's pieces— a ceramic pitcher by Georges Jouve and a lacy marble vessel by Sottsass—are displayed on Pierre Bonnefille's coffee tables, which can easily be used together or separately.

ABOVE: The library's windows overlook the garden. Its walls are painted a warm, soothing shade of gray, a slightly deeper tone than the one used elsewhere in the house. The photograph that hangs above Piero Lissoni's sofa is by Philippe Ramette; by featuring himself in the scene, he mocks power with a symbolically derisive gesture.

RIGHT: Natural stone is used on the ground floor. A 1950s piece by Ettore Sottsass serves as a desk. Hans-Peter Feldmann's pictures of squinting figures, *Les Loucheurs*, are representative of the work of this artist, who humorously repurposes traditional canvases.

BELOW, LEFT: Livening up the library, decorative objects are randomly combined with books on the shelves. In its own distinctive idiom, Marc Newson's wicker chair combines organic forms with Japanese craftsmanship.

BELOW, RIGHT: In the third-floor bedroom, the bed is glimpsed through the branches forming the back of Andrea Branzi's "Animali Domestici" bench. Alessandro Mendini's stacked boxes in lacquer, laminate, ceramic, and artisanal paint are used for storage.

FACING PAGE: Located on the second floor overlooking the street, the living room has a stone mantelpiece that serves as a focal point. The room features a blend of styles: a gilt-framed mirror beside an Arte Povera floor lamp by Andrea Branzi; an Iranian carpet below Sottsass vases; nineteenth-century paneling behind a "Favella" chair by the Campana brothers.

BY LES INVALIDES

Nothing is concealed in Sylvie Blanchet's apartment.
An interior architect, she welcomed the challenge of treating
the space like a loft. She eliminated walls and stripped out color,
creating a wall of glass that acts as a screen. Her well-appointed
bedroom is reminiscent of a suite in a luxury hotel.

LEFT: The living-room carpet, based on a cubist design by Eileen Gray, harmonizes with the building's 1930s architecture. Thierry d'Istria, one of Sylvie's partners, designed the tank-shaped bud vase displayed on a metal table from Lieux.

FACING PAGE: An essential component of the overall decorative scheme, the library shelving with its lacquered surfaces separates the bedroom and the entrance from the living room. An unusually tall Eiffel-style table lends a distinctive touch to the corner office space. The nearby chairs are by Thierry d'Istria, and the one in the foreground is signed by Ron Arad. The original wood floor was simply sanded and stained taupe.

ABOVE: The frames of the French doors are painted black, as are the mountings for the glass panels in the kitchen overlooking the main room. Stretched midway across the windowpanes, translucent linen panels filter the light without hiding the view. Armchairs and sofas by Gerrit Rietveld and floor lamps by Andrée Putman are combined in a harmonious interplay of angles and curves.

LEFT: Three feet above the floor, a khaki-colored shelf runs around the large space that encompasses the living and dining rooms; it is used to display paintings and photographs. Two-tone drapery panels extend the line, avoiding visual interruption.

RIGHT: On the dining-room side, a long table covered with lightly tinted glass welcomes guests. In a spirit of playfulness, the chairs are unmatched and the eighteenth-century mirror is flanked by a bevy of PVC convex mirrors.

BELOW, LEFT: Behind a glass wall, the kitchen is open to the living room. The space is sophisticated in the extreme, bedecked with elegant crystal chandeliers.

BELOW, RIGHT: Jacques Bosser's photograph shows Su Tilley, the muse and model of the painter Lucien Freud, coiffed and made up as if for a Kabuki performance. The bronzes are by Philippe Anthonioz.

PAGES 92–93: Behind mirrored doors that assure privacy, the bed stands in the middle of the room to provide the best view of the garden's trees. It features the distinctive shade of orange of the Hermès boxes that are randomly stacked on top of the cupboard.

NEAR LES INVALIDES

In contrast to the exposed beams and traditional country furniture of her luxury Alpine resort, Les Fermes de Marie, Jocelyne Sibuet chose a traditional Haussmann-era building as a retreat from her duties at the hotel group she manages so expertly. She wanted traditional moldings, old wooden floors, and plenty of sunshine all day long.

LEFT: A combined living and dining room share the same space. The taupe of the walls, accented by the white ceiling, creates an impression of unity, punctuated by graphic black alcoves. The furnishings, as well as Joseph Klibansky's painting on a photograph, all convey the concept of urban modernity.

ABOVE: A sense of restraint pervades the entire space with its straight lines, lacquered surfaces, chrome and leather, a painting by the Italian artist Monti, and an illuminated rock crystal sculpture.

PAGES 96–97: A balcony runs the length of the apartment, which is located on the top floor, with no other building obstructing its outlook. It is oriented east–west with windowed doors offering a view of the Eiffel Tower. The bedroom, which can be seen beyond the fireplace, is accessed through the living room. It features a silky carpet, satin draperies, and velvet cushions, all expressing a taste for harmony and femininity.

RUE DES SAINTS-PÈRES

A sundrenched living room in a nineteenth-century building with tall windows overlooks a corner of this street in Saint-Germain-des-Prés. In Stéphane Olivier's home, as in his gallery, furniture made from precious woods displays his favorite collector's items.

LEFT: Beyond the corridor leading to the bedroom, a door opens into the living room. Three Brazilian rosewood cabinets with adjustable shelves give structure to the room. The subtly shaded veins of the rare wood lend a note of exoticism. The walls are painted two colors, a luminous chalk white and a very masculine khaki. A few collector's items are on display, including a nineteenth-century wig holder of mercurized glass and a painting school plaster cast. The collector's chair is signed by Barnaba Fornasetti.

FACING PAGE: Discovered by Stéphane in New York and brought home in his luggage, these traffic signals have become lighting fixtures, mockingly displayed next to a nineteenth-century sculpture. An iconic piece, the Bikini chair, made of black-lacquered metal and leather, is by Charles Eames.

ABOVE: The living room overlooking the legendary rue des Saints-Pères features a distinctive piece of furniture: a teak coffee table in the restrained Danish modern style of the 1950s. Its components can be disassembled and rearranged at will depending on the desired shape. The bookshelf holds little treasures from his own personal museum collection: a Roman glass plate, a bronze lamp by the Lalannes, and a Chinese vase from the twelfth century BCE.

LEFT: In one of those fleeting effects that captures the eye, a window is reflected in a photograph by Jean-Baptiste Huyn, showing two hands holding open the pages of a Coptic bible.

ABOVE, LEFT: Vintage furniture in the bedroom: the Verner Panton chair is an original plywood version; a 1960s Danish sideboard serves as a chest.

ABOVE, RIGHT: Displayed on the marble mantelpiece, a collection of plaster flayed men and models recalls a traditional cabinet of curiosities. They are dramatized by the lighting, the play of shadows, and the reflections.

RIGHT: With its mélange of styles, the bedroom embraces some appealing details: bedside lamps fashioned from Regency carved wood columns topped with picture lights, a bronze convex mirror by Hervé Van der Straeten, and an eighteenth-century Italian painted chair.

THE SOUL OF
A COLLECTOR

THE ART OF MATCHING
A COLLECTION TO A HOME

PAGE 102: Produced in Europe and the United States from the 1970s onward, originally in metal and then in plastic, Jean-Bernard Hebey's vacuum cleaner collection includes tank and standing models.

FACING PAGE, CLOCKWISE FROM TOP LEFT:
A 1950s Adnet lamp is displayed on the mantelpiece together with nineteenth-century Indian heads fashioned from wax.

A table set with hand-painted plates, a tablecloth, and napkins with embroidery based on the designs of François Daneck.

Draped over a chair stamped by Brian et Maigret (1810), a silk velvet train embroidered with gold for the Countess of Boigne.

Microphones dating from the 1930s and 1940s, with streamlined grilles, and a Radio Nurse radio transmitter by Isamu Noguchi (in the foreground) and a Philips "pancake" loud speaker (in the middle ground), both in Bakelite.

Perhaps collecting is a way to tame an object. We slip these treasures into our lives, wondering what stories they could tell. Some collectors start at a very young age. One began subscribing to the famous auction house's *Gazette de l'Hôtel Drouot* at the age of fourteen; another was devouring books on art nouveau; and a third experienced a revelation during his first visit to a museum. A taste for collecting takes over; tentative at first, it soon becomes more compelling. With the passage of time, random encounters and curiosity combine to do the rest. Traveling, stepping through an antique shop's door, following an auction sale—every one of these acts can lead to a new acquisition. Furniture, paintings, sculptures, fossils, and photographs all lure the collector's eye, suggesting myriad possibilities. The collector's sensibilities become heightened, and selectivity becomes essential.

A recollection of bygone days, a walk through a souk, a Saturday whiled away at a flea market, the appeal of an innovative design, a news article—a collector is always on the lookout to add to his hoard. Once brought home, the new treasure, objet d'art, or piece of furniture mingles with the existing furnishings, finding its proper place gradually, with a sense of balance and harmony. Disparate styles intermingle, as do civilizations, periods, and genres. Close-knit ties develop; there is a kind of complicity between the collector and his possessions. It is easy to forget that a chair once had a different owner, or that a painting or a table used to belong to someone else. All these articles are gradually absorbed into a new environment.

Some collectors rethink the entire house in order to establish this dialogue and create a welcoming environment for the collection. Walls may be painted in period colors, moldings and *boiseries* accented with gold. A room may be altered with shelves installed to store industrially designed articles. A piece of furniture may be designed or appropriated to safely hold a few treasured ceramics or terra-cottas. A wondrously elaborate and fantastically sculpted Renaissance mantelpiece might be the perfect spot for a display. This is how collectors reveal themselves; their choices reflect their inner selves like self-portraits. These connoisseurs take profound pleasure in the memories and recollections evoked by the objects they live with every waking moment. They are eloquent reminders of past experiences.

IN SURESNES

A house in the Bauhaus style harbors one of the most astonishing
collections of industrially designed objects imaginable.
They testify to the twentieth century's visionary modernity.
The owner, Jean-Bernard Hebey, is a media professional who
is endlessly inquisitive about the aesthetics of domesticity.

LEFT: Rare turntables are displayed in an office; Oskar Schlemmer's 1927 model in red and John Vassos's turntable for RCA in its Haliburton metal carrying case. Mounted on podiums are three outboard motors, one of which was designed by Brook Stevens. On the shelves stand plastic turntables and slot-fed record players produced in Italy during the 1970s, the "My First Sony" series, and the first Teppaz portable record players.

ABOVE: "Womb Chair," Saarinen's armchair designed for Knoll; a model of a Boeing 707 in cast aluminum; a "Sofono Spacemaster" electric heater, designed by Ralph Ormiston in 1959; a painting by Hervé di Rosa; Achille Castiglioni's "Arc" floor lamp, 1962.

RIGHT: The metal piers were designed by Jean-Bernard Hebey to hold the entire Domus collection. The daybed is by Mies Van der Rohe. On display is an inventory of vintage items, including a sprinkler, a vacuum cleaner, a 1970 coffee mill, and a poultry incubator.

BELOW, LEFT: The shelves hold archival material and documentation on the work of Jean-Bernard Hebey. In the back of the room stands a grouping of fans and blenders dating from the 1920s through the 1970s.

BELOW, RIGHT: An American Hamilton Beach blender for making milk shakes, dating from the 1950s, and an electric mixer and can opener.

FACING PAGE: In the living room stands a "Marshmallow" sofa by George Nelson and a grouping of film spools from the 1930s. Displayed on the dividing wall are fruit squeezers shaped like parrots, while hanging on the wall are charcoal drawings by Jean-Charles Blais.

IN THE MARAIS

In the sumptuous setting of a seventeenth-century *hôtel particulier* (town house), built on an imposing scale, a knowledgeable collector skillfully displays his treasures throughout the residence. It is a remarkably eclectic array, gleaned from auction houses in Paris, London, and New York, and guided by one unshakable principle—only objects of impeccable quality should be purchased.

ABOVE: In the dining room, a work by Doug and Mike Starn stands out against a leather-paneled wall. A bronze statue of General Hoche by Dalou is displayed on a stand by Eugène Gaillard. The carpet is by Garouste et Bonetti, produced for Christian Lacroix's couture house, the floor lamp is by Diego Giacometti, and in the entrance hall stands a 1930 sculpture by Anton Prinner.

TOP, RIGHT: The lofty walls of the living room are decorated with mirrors and tapestries; the series depicting the Liberal Arts was woven in Bruges in the seventeenth century. A wooden sculpture by Ossip Zadkine stands near an Indo-Portuguese cabinet on which a figurine from Sierra Leone is displayed. The sofa is by Scarpa; the floor lamp is signed by Lebovici.

BOTTOM, RIGHT: Lebrun's 1654 painting *Susannah and the Elders* once hung in the old Court of Appeal in the Palais de Justice in Paris. Displayed on an aluminum and wooden chest designed by Françoise Sée are works by Anton Prinner and Lichtenstein, and a lamp by Serge Manzon. An eleventh-century Indian sculpture and a horse by Senoufo stand on the coffee table.

BELOW: The salon is furnished in part with chairs designed by Warren Platner for Knoll; an Aztec stone sculpture of a water goddess stands atop a coffee table.

PAGES 112–13: Painted by José Maria Sert, the martyrdoms of Saint John and Saint Peter impose their baroque aesthetic in one of the bedrooms. A chair by Rateau stands in front of an eighteenth-century lacquer secretary from Japan. A lacquered table dominates the center of the room, topped by a portrait bust of Khafra, a Fourth Dynasty pharaoh.

TOP, RIGHT: *Boiserie* panels, the only ones ever designed by the painter Lévy Dhurmer, cover the bedroom's two thousand square feet (200 m²) of walls. A statue from Easter Island that once belonged to Paul Éluard stands on the mantelpiece.

BOTTOM, RIGHT: On the top floor of this town house, beneath the twenty-six-foot (8 m) roofline, a passage leads from the bedroom to the library. On the mantelpiece stands a ceramic piece from Mexico's Jalisco province, about two thousand years old. A bronze by Bourdelle, one of the figures in his Montauban monument, is reflected in a mirror by Jacques Grüber. Maurice Denis's *Descent from the Cross* (1901) hangs on the wall.

BELOW: By the bed, a desk and chair by Eugène Gaillard are paired together. On the wall hangs Armand Point's allegory *April* and a portrait of Jean-Gabriel Domergue's wife.

LEFT: In one of the bedrooms decorated with trompe l'oeil marble walls is *Eloquence*, a bronze by Bourdelle, which was one of the components of the monument to General Alvear in Buenos Aires. A sculpture by Lobi stands on a pair of nesting tables.

BELOW: On a Lévy Dhurmer desk in the collector's bedroom, Tiffany lamps illuminate an African mask and an Egyptian sculpture from the Thirteenth Dynasty. Beneath a Venetian scene stand a table by Majorelle and a bronze head by Manolo; displayed below a rare landscape by Eugène Carrière is a bronze by Jules Desbois, who worked in Rodin's studio.

NEAR THE HÔTEL DE VILLE

Painstakingly remodeled in the Empire style, this apartment boasts exquisite gold-leaf mirrors and moldings. It is the haunt of Pierre-Jean Chalençon, a collector of Napoleonic memorabilia, so fanatical that he will happily hop on a flight to attend a distant auction and enhance his already vast collection.

LEFT: This sofa and chair of gilt wood were created by Georges Jacob for the emperor's imperial lodge in the Tuileries. The marble bust of Napoleon was sculpted by Antoine-Denis Chaudet in 1808.

FACING PAGE: In the entrance hall is a portrait of the emperor intended for the Musée Napoléon, commissioned by Vivant Denon from Michel Martin Drolling. Sèvres vases given by Napoleon to Baron Regnault d'Angely stand behind Brian et Maigret armchairs, upholstered with motifs from the bedroom of Napoleon's son, the king of Rome.

PAGES 118–19: In a salon are pieces signed by Marcian: armchairs from the Château de Fontainebleau and a sofa made for Marshal Mortier, flanked by marble columns from the Besteigui collection topped by bronze vases commissioned by Napoleon for the birth of the king of Rome.

ABOVE, LEFT: "Nubian feet," a detail of the classical legs of a painted and gilded wood state bed in the Egyptian Revival style. It was produced for King Jerome of Westphalia.

ABOVE, RIGHT: Beneath the baldachin, which has been restored with fresh gold leaf, the Egyptian Revival state bed that belonged to King Jerome of Westphalia is signed by Jacob. The armchair and side chair come from the collections of Marshal Mortier. The painting by Robert Lefebvre, *Love Sharpening His Arrows*, was exhibited in the Salon of 1798.

LEFT: Still in its original gilt wood frame, ornamented with the imperial eagle, this is a portrait of Empress Marie-Louise by Baron Gérard. Books bound in gold-trimmed leather, purchased at an auction, came from Napoleon's library at Malmaison.

RIGHT: The arms of Napoleon III are displayed in the bedroom alongside a portrait of Bonaparte by Baron Gros and ceremonial fasces from the coronation. In the oval frames, the emperor is depicted in his coronation robes. The campaign chair belonged to Marshal Davout.

BELOW, LEFT: The matching sofa and armchair in the entrance, signed by the cabinetmakers Brian et Maigret in 1810, were given by Napoleon to the Turkish ruler, the Sultan of the Sublime Porte. On the wall hangs a painting of the emperor in his coronation robes and an 1808 Aubusson tapestry.

BELOW, RIGHT: The bust of Napoleon in biscuit porcelain from the Imperial Manufactory in Sèvres is dated 1810. The gilt bronze diadem is by Thomire.

PAGES 122–23: Beneath the gaze of a life-size Napoleon (5 ft. 6 in./1.68 m), made from painted cardboard and inspired by Isabey, a table is set with glasses and plates bearing the arms of Talleyrand.

NEAR THE PALAIS-ROYAL

Tucked away in one of the most charming passages in Paris, this apartment belongs to the gallery owner Pierre Passebon. His selection of furnishings and objects, mingling civilizations and eras, creates a self-portrait revealing an insatiable curiosity, which he satisfies with travel and fresh encounters.

LEFT: The living room's decor features a dramatic checkerboard backdrop in the colors of Siena, an allusion to the civic competition known as the Palio. Flanking the stone fireplace, which is reminiscent of the sculptures in the Bomarzo gardens, are a screen by Burne-Jones, photographs by Dieter Appelt, and armchairs by Carlo Molino. Patrice Dangel's silver gilt irons resemble fangs. The coffee table is by Eyre de Lanux, the American art-deco artist. In the corner stands a nineteenth-century Italian table on which a trio of figures is displayed: a bronze head by Max Klinger, *Awakening* by Lord Leighton, and an eighteenth-century flayed man.

ABOVE: *The Hero*, a 1925 bronze by Marcel Landowski. There is a striking play of colors in the feathered Amazonian Indian headdresses and the Napoleon III coral tiara, a gift from a friend.

RIGHT: In the dining room, a folding table by Jean-Michel Frank, with armchairs and a vitrine by Paul Poiret (with Atelier Martine). Champagne bucket by Marcial Berro; photograph by Matthew Barney; *Amazon* and *Centaur* statues by Franz von Stuck.

BELOW, LEFT: Displayed atop a pair of "corrugated" mahogany Louis XVI chests stamped by Moreau are plaster sculptures by Gio Ponti and gilt bronze Turkish finials. In the background, a screen made from felt collage is signed by Jean-Émile Laboureur.

BELOW, RIGHT: Whimsical wire chairs by Madeleine Castaing purchased at the estate sale of her property in Lèves. The neoclassical plaster figure is in keeping with the building's Directoire style.

FACING PAGE: Fashioned from ceramic and metal, a table by Jouve is used to display a lamp by Ingo Maurer. The steel armchair dates from the early nineteenth century; the mirror is Venetian.

BY THE FLEA MARKET IN SAINT-OUEN

Treasures gleaned from Madagascar, Africa, and Asia mix with novel creations inspired by exotic voyages. Welcome to the home of François Daneck, a dealer in curiosities whose discoveries have made this house his own. Everything on display is for sale under the "Africa Concept" label.

LEFT: On a console fashioned from straw marquetry work are lamps covered with zebra skin, ammonite fossils, and paper nautilus and pecten shells. The bronze elephant is by Yves Gaumetou, the fluted ceramic vase with white gold leaf by Antonio da Silva; a collection of insects and butterflies mingle with taxidermy antelope, lion cub, and buffalo heads, and "Melo" lighting fixtures made from shells.

ABOVE: In the bedroom stands a 1940s secretary, topped with a "Punu" mask from the Congo and an eighteenth-century Chinese marionette. A stool covered with ocelot skin stands in front, alongside an *Oreotragus saltatrix* taxidermy antelope, and an armchair covered with tanned sheepskin. On the wall are a ballpoint pen drawing by Augustin Cardenas and framed colonial banknotes.

RIGHT: An armchair covered in zebra skin and leather with an "Orileg" throw stands in front of curtains of "Kuba" cotton on a zebra patchwork rug. Behind is a chest covered in iguana skin and a colonial pedestal, on which stand sculptures by the Asmat tribe of Papua New Guinea.

BELOW, LEFT: In the dining room are armchairs covered in python skin, a sideboard incorporating the horns of the humped cattle known as zebu, and an ostrich egg lighting fixture. On the wall hangs a bronze relief by Albert Jouanneault, created for the 1931 World's Fair.

BELOW, RIGHT: On the wall behind a Siberian tiger is a Bubale antelope skull electroplated with nickel; a woven shield from the Congo; and wall fixtures made from ostrich eggs. The painting is by Roger Nivelt.

FACING PAGE: Standing by the door is a screen fashioned from various exotic woods, mother-of-pearl, shells, and patinated copper. Above the door are tiger shark jaws. The room also features a Burchell zebra head on the wall; a marsh-dwelling Black Lechwe antelope; albino and blue peacocks, and a stool covered in zebra-skin patchwork.

NEAR THE OPÉRA

Sacha Walckhoff, the creative director of the Maison Christian Lacroix, lives near the Opéra. His apartment is steeped in the atmosphere of the nineteenth century. Over time, its furnishings and interiors have become a harmonious ensemble with a uniquely Parisian sense of style.

LEFT: In the kitchen, an early twentieth-century Syrian marriage chest with mother-of-pearl and eggshell inlays adorns one wall, alongside a photograph by Alexander Sy Meyer. The vintage Habitat table dates from the 1980s and around it stands a Charles Eames chair and a Tolix armchair.

FACING PAGE: A zebra leaping from the entrance wall adds a surrealist touch. The steel bench is by Maria Pergay (early 1970s); chair with *passementeries* and fabric by Sacha Walckhoff and Rodrigo Almeida for Christian Lacroix; stools by Knoll; floor lamp by Janette Laverriere (late 1940s); and chairs by Maarten Baas and Big Game.

PAGES 134–35: At the entrance to the living room, the metallic chair is by Marcel Wanders, the silver-plated stool is by Pedro Friedeberg and the contemporary Danish stool by Mogens Lassen. The 1950s ceramic tables are by Capron and the sofa made with Rodrigo Almeida. The decorative panel with classical cityscape, rugs, and fabrics are by Sacha Walckhoff for Christian Lacroix.

ABOVE, LEFT: "Forum" and "Butterfly Parade" plates. Cast-iron place settings are by the Conran Shop; "Les Endiablés" glasses are from the Cristallerie de Saint-Louis.

ABOVE, RIGHT: Beneath a photograph by Mohamed Bourouissa (Kamel Mennour Gallery) stand three tables by Mathieu Mategot. The ceramic jug is by Georges Jouve (1950s), the double chair by Rolf Sachs (Ammann Gallery in Cologne), and the lamp by Gismondi.

LEFT: In the dining room hangs a photograph taken by Véronique Ellena when she was living in the Villa Medici, one of a series of works on the homeless. The 1950s metal and leather table is by Adnet, the curtain is cut velvet "Riviera"; the 1940s lamp is by Boris Lacroix.

RIGHT: The cattle skull nailed to the living-room door was purchased in Miami. Necklaces, chains, and pendants—from Christian Lacroix, Hermès, and the flea market—are draped over the horns.

BELOW, LEFT: In the library stand shelving units by MUJI, topped by a collection of boxes by Marcel Wanders for Habitat. The stools are by Charlotte Perriand and rock sculptures by Cazenove.

BELOW, RIGHT: *Vanilla*, a multimedia work by Daniel Firman, shows a plastic figure enveloped by tires; the 1950s armchair is covered in matte and shiny velvet; the lamp is by Pierre Disderot.

AT THE TROCADÉRO

With its fantastical array of colors and fabrics, the apartment of
designer Krystina Dwernicka embraces travel souvenirs, cunningly
repurposed objects, and a folkloric spirit that happily blend
together under her watchful eye. A gently familial aura pervades
this nostalgic setting.

LEFT: Suzani embroideries from Uzbekistan; bolsters from the Istanbul bazaar; Indian cushions; armchairs upholstered with a folkloric woolen print used to make traditional skirts in Poland—enthusiasm for fabrics is evident in the living room. The coffee table of blue Plexiglas features blue scarab motifs; the floor lamps were discovered in Warsaw.

ABOVE: On an eighteenth-century Polish chest, hand-painted with traditional designs, stands a vase covered with fabric and mounted as a lamp base. The portrait above is of the Duchess of Dino, Talleyrand's beloved.

PAGES 140–41: The bedroom is a riot of color with Uzbekistan Suzani embroideries on the wall as well as the bed. A glass-covered frame holds an eighteenth-century child's frock worn by an ancestor. Michal Zaborowski's gouache highlighted with gold leaf hangs over the console. Statues of the Virgin were collected in France and Brazil. The Polish furniture is handcrafted.

RIGHT: The table has legs in the form of dolphins; on it stands a sculpture by Pierre-Marie Lejeune, a close friend of Niki de Saint-Phalle. The portraits of children are by Grzegorz Smigielski.

BELOW, LEFT: In the kitchen, there are books, magazines, and guides to leaf through while enjoying a snack, and a collection of vividly colored butterflies. The table was found in Poland.

BELOW, RIGHT: In the entrance hall, one wall is covered with Delft-style tiles, reminiscent of those that decorated the staircase of the Nieborów Palace. The marquetry table is nineteenth-century Russian, and the traditional Polish horses are handcrafted out of wicker. The portrait is believed to depict Madame de Montespan.

FACING PAGE: The stool is upholstered in Suzani embroidery; the novel coffee table with three tops was discovered in Biarritz. Other notable features are the luminous metal columnar sculpture mounted with glass bottles and the blue resin chair by Pierre-Marie Lejeune.

DESIGNERS AND CREATORS

COMBINING LIVING SPACES
AND PLACES OF EXPERIMENTATION

PAGE 144: A graphic
composition in black and
white: a juxtaposition of
metal coffee tables with two
lamps fashioned from rattan
and tissue paper by Paola
Navone.

FACING PAGE, CLOCKWISE
FROM TOP LEFT:
A study in contrasting curves
and angles, a sculpture
punctuates the wall's uniform
surface.

A linear metal console sports
a bronze lamp printed with
a mesh motif by Christian
Liaigre.

A kitchen counter is reflected
in the surface of a stainless-
steel cupboard.

The spare lines of a sofa
contrast with the curve of the
walls.

Saint-Germain-des-Prés is one of those neighborhoods that has always attracted designers and creators. Other areas are less central, retaining a Bohemian aura that has a continuing appeal. Wherever designers choose to live, they make their homes into places of experimentation, skillfully mingling eras and styles. They depend upon the invaluable assistance of Parisian crafts-men—none of this creativity would be possible without the contributions of accomplished woodworkers, cabinetmakers, metal craftsmen, and ceramicists. Once the overall decorative scheme is defined and the design concept is clar-ified, the space is reconfigured and opened out, furnishings are rethought, areas are repurposed, and windows are enlarged to provide abundant natu-ral light. The materials selected complement the architecture. Great attention to almost imperceptible detail is an expression of understated luxury. Colors are a key element. The same flooring is often used throughout the space to create a sense of unity and accentuate the effect of perspective. A single tone for the walls may create a mood of balance and calm. One artist–decorator, inspired by his travels, often switches among a variety of color schemes that he associates with exotic escapes: yellow, turquoise, fuchsia, and gold trans-form and transfigure the furnishings. An interior decorator combines his or her own furnishings with those of other designers, adding treasures gleaned from voyages throughout the world. Vivid, exotic fabrics are tossed on tables and sofas, changing the ambience of a living room or library with the simplest of gestures. The apartment provides a setting for vases made by Japanese and Italian craftsmen in glass or porcelain. These creative artists live surrounded by a myriad of objects and images that influence their own work, blending daily routine with inspired innovation. They embrace all these roles, designing their apartments with the same dedication they apply to their artistic creations.

IN THE HEART OF PARIS

Interior architect and designer Sarah Lavoine opens up
some rooms in order to configure others. She structures spaces
with graphic black accents, adding touches of intense color,
as if composing a painting. These samples of her work are drawn
from three different apartments.

LEFT: The walls of this nineteenth-century apartment were demolished and replaced by pillars that support the ceiling; a tall mirror shows their reflection, reinforcing the impression of an artist's studio. Jean Prouvé's metal daybed fits naturally into this ensemble.

FACING PAGE: The dining space is a subtle symphony of grays and blacks. The simple lines of the metal table, the Polaroids by Marc Lavoine, and a photograph by Valérie Knight, which transforms a tiny bonsai into a mighty tree, all contribute to the setting. The oak benches, a simple linear statement, are by Sarah Lavoine.

LEFT: The living room's decor offers a mélange of styles and modernity. The mirror frame is painted deep black, and the austere lines of Nathalie Decoster's sculpture and Charlotte Perriand's armchairs contrast with the exuberance of the nineteenth-century mantelpiece.

BELOW, LEFT: For the library walls, Sarah Lavoine chose Indian Blue, one of a range of tones she created. The doors are emphasized with black paint.

BELOW, RIGHT: Skillful use of black lends structure and style to the kitchen, creating visual unity between the furniture, painted floor, and doors. Just a single note of intense color, the vivid green of the table catches the eye like a chic accessory.

LEFT: Fabrics, *boiseries*, and linens form a visual harmony: the bedroom's subtle color scheme ranges from charcoal gray to deep black. A painted wood structure serves as shelf and headboard.

BELOW, LEFT: Conveying Sarah Lavoine's distinctive style, the dining room is painted a bold sunflower yellow with black trim and white highlights, reminiscent of a modernist painting. The open door allows a glimpse of the living room and the library beyond.

BELOW, RIGHT: Seen from the living room, the rooms open spaciously from one to the next. The enfilade is punctuated by doorways with cut-off corners, all framed in black. The mirrors surrounding the window reflect the light and the view of the street outside.

PAGES 152–53: To create a living-room area within an open space, Sarah Lavoine built an oak framework with glass panels that are hung with sheer linen curtains.

ABOVE, LEFT: Tucked beneath the eaves in what was once the servants' floor, a bed is recessed in an alcove. The striped design of the floor echoes the linear contrast between the exposed beams and the ceiling.

ABOVE, RIGHT: The beige tonalities and white touches of the living room contrast with the floorboards in a striking graphic effect. Deep "Super Box" sofas face the television, which is enclosed in a cabinet that incorporates shelves.

LEFT: Sarah Lavoine used subtle gray tones for the dining nook, designed as a living space. It is part of the kitchen, which is separated from the dining room by glass panels.

TOP, LEFT: A cabinetmaker followed Sarah's design for the bedroom, crafting a built-in unit made from stained oak; it includes bookshelves, closets, and a central console. The structure frames the bed, whose white linens stand out against the deep-red walls.

BOTTOM, LEFT: The living room's beige is used again on the walls of the entrance hall; a solid band of white creates the illusion of paneling and draws attention to the graceful curves of a Louis XVI daybed set beneath a baroque mirror. It harmonizes flawlessly with the contemporary architecture and the dark-stained floorboards.

BELOW: The rigorous simplicity of the bathroom melds the austere and traditional. The old-fashioned bathtub, resting on clawed lion feet, is painted charcoal gray. In striking contrast, the walls and floor are done in beige *tadelakt*, a traditional Moroccan plaster finish.

NEAR SAINT-GERMAIN-DES-PRÉS

In a building dating from the 1930s, the artist and decorator
Serge Olivares has painted the walls of his apartment
with vividly contrasting colors that interplay with light to
create a theatrical backdrop for his designs.

LEFT: In the living room, broad vertical stripes alternate in orange and fuchsia. The furniture and decorative accents reveal a pronounced affinity for operatic drama, bullfights, and uncanny metamorphoses. A Venetian sofa is upholstered in velvet, and a sculpted wooden chair is covered with astrakhan and transformed into a bull; taxidermy birds perch on the floor lamps. The wall-to-wall carpet flaunts a pink panther pattern.

ABOVE: The walls of the corridor leading to the bedroom and studio are painted black, and the ceiling is covered in gold leaf. Ethnic images, a mix of favorite colors, an antique *passementerie* curtain tieback, satin, and feathers are tacked up as if in a fashion trend book.

RIGHT: Creating an intriguing optical effect, some of the bedroom's paintings and sculptures are hung upside down, a reminder that we see the world differently from a reclining position. Pillows are heaped generously on a faux tiger skin, evoking an Eastern harem.

BELOW, LEFT: The living room features another vivid color—a golden yellow that matches the costume worn by singer Luis Mariano in the operetta *La Belle de Cadix.* Serge Olivares used it to cover a Louis XV chair.

BELOW, RIGHT: Standing prominently by the entrance hall's turquoise wall, a mannequin from the 1930s, bedecked in butterfly wings and covered with gold leaf, is a welcoming angel to greet arriving guests.

ABOVE: Humor, preciosity, and historic references: a Gustavian table is covered in gold leaf; a hanging lamp has been patiently adorned with three thousand Swarovski crystals; and a "Devil" ottoman is upholstered in velvet and elaborate antique *passementerie*.

TOP, RIGHT: Another reference to the bullring: a "Toreador" chair in jet-embroidered leather stands on a carpet embroidered with a sun stitched in gold thread.

BOTTOM, RIGHT: Serge Olivares works in the studio at the end of the hall. It is bursting with drawings, portraits, masks, fans, photographs, statuettes, and figurines—all sources of inspiration.

BY SAINT-GERMAIN-DES-PRÉS

Designer and interior architect Agnès Comar took full advantage of this former office space when she remodeled it for an apartment. She demolished the partitions, creating an enfilade of rooms where each space opens directly onto the next with no doors between, creating a lovely effect of light and flow.

LEFT: In the living room and throughout the apartment, two colors are used to create a sense of unity. The walls are painted chestnut brown, and white resin is used for the floors. Here and there, a table, chair, sculpture, or the lining of a curtain adds a lively note of contrast.

FACING PAGE: Just like the other rooms, the bedroom opens onto the enfilade that extends the entire length of the windowed facade, receiving abundant natural light. There are no jarring notes to interfere with the decor's graceful balance, which is emphasized by the simplicity and pure lines of the furnishings.

PAGES 162–63: The kitchen doubles as a dining room. Two polished steel bank counters are set end to end, echoing the gleaming presence of Jacques Martinez's sculptured armoire. Continuing the theme, the bistro banquette is upholstered in metallic fabric, and the chairs are made from folded sheet metal.

RIGHT: The apartment's rooms open onto one another, each with ceiling-high windows. The living room is followed by the kitchen–dining room, then the study, bedroom, and bathroom.

BELOW: In the living room, the white resin flooring that covers the entire apartment is visible on either side of the wool and silk carpet and the velvet sofa designed by Agnès Comar. Throughout, the light is filtered by the honeycomb blinds.

LEFT: The bathroom is designed as a living space with sophisticated touches of gleaming metal and reflections from the old-fashioned bathtub's shining exterior finish. The lacy cabinet is by Pucci di Rossi.

BELOW, LEFT: The same chestnut used in the rest of the apartment gives the bathroom the air of a boudoir, an impression enhanced by the lacquered-wood and glass table that contains the washbasin. A gilt metal mirror stands out from the wall. In keeping with a setting characterized by elegant simplicity and refined detail, the curtain is lined with absinthe-green fabric.

BELOW, RIGHT: The rule is reversed in the bedroom, where the walls are painted white to capture the light, and the carpet, cushions, and bedspread are chestnut brown. A striking photograph by Swiss artists Peter Fischli and David Weiss accents the wall, harmonizing flawlessly with the rest of the decor.

NEAR THE CHAMP-DE-MARS

To create a sense of unity between the former servants' quarters and the main floor of a nineteenth-century building, transforming them into a duplex, interior architect Pierre Yovanovitch tore down walls. He reconfigured spaces and volumes, making skillful use of stone and untreated wood to establish a sense of profound, yet discreet luxury.

LEFT: The living room opens onto the library. Recessed in the wall, a supremely simple fireplace in "Imperial Grey" stone is centered over a bench that runs the panel's entire length. In a pleasing harmony of curves and materials, a solid oak sofa, ceramic tables, and hemp carpeting designed by the architect create a balance between asceticism and sophistication.

ABOVE: From the entryway, steps carved from solid stone lead to three upstairs bedrooms. A glass panel serves as a banister at the top and closes off the staircase, leaving an open view.

PAGES 168–69: This intimate living room with its double exposure has windows overlooking the garden; old oak floorboards are used here, as in the other rooms. The metal and cork sofa is by Pierre Yovanovitch, and works by Philippe Cognée (Galerie Daniel Templon) hang on the walls.

LEFT: The library, custom designed in solid pine, also serves as a dining room. Leather chairs designed by Enzo Mari for Hermès are arranged around Pierre Yovanovitch's metal table.

BELOW, LEFT: One of the two upstairs guestrooms features original exposed beams. Each is designed like a hotel suite with its own bath and dressing room. A painting by Billy Childish (Lehmann Maupin Gallery) introduces the colors of the American South.

BELOW, RIGHT: The gray hues of slate in a guest bathroom. The shower opens into a sky-dome in the roof. The natural light creates the effect of rain when the water is flowing.

FACING PAGE: The kitchen is in matte lacquered wood and Basaltina with custom finishing. The 1950s-style backsplash was designed by the architect and executed by ceramic artist Armelle Benoit.

PORTE DES LILAS

In a former factory where they often lived surrounded by rubble, artists Pierre Commoy and Gilles Blanchard built a working and living space for themselves. This pop-art world is suffused with color, illusion, and allusions to the themes of travel and chance encounters.

LEFT: A playful tone is set by a 1960s Canadian chest, its drawers studded with nails. A throng of figurines and dolls—ranging from Michael Jackson and Justin Bieber to Brigitte Bardot and Sylvie Vartan—cluster beneath James Bidgood's work, a still from the film *Pink Narcissus*.

FACING PAGE: Narrow steps lead to an upstairs passageway that runs the length of the living room and suggests the deck of a ship. It leads to the bar referred to as "Bar de la Marine" (Marine Bar). The small opening in the downstairs wall echoes the shipboard theme. A spangled Eiffel Tower created by Pierre et Gilles, an Afghan war rug woven with submachine-gun, tank, and helicopter motifs, a garland of plastic flowers, and life-size renderings of superheroes Goldorak and Batman combine to create a fantastical, transgressive decor.

PAGES 174–75: The dining room is bursting with innumerable allusions in a dazzling kaleidoscope of colors: the television and countless fetishistic objects are displayed as if on an altar in Thailand. A garland of plastic flowers purchased in Turkey hangs over the window. On the floor is a vinyl sheet printed with a children's game. The wall surrounding the archway leading to the living room is lavishly covered in spangles, creating a jewel-like effect.

ABOVE, LEFT: Pierre and Gilles have covered the wall and vaulted ceiling of the hall leading to the Bar de la Marine with spangles. They added a table found in Barbès, in Paris, which has been topped with sailor and mermaid figurines.

ABOVE, RIGHT: Reminiscent of a giant porthole, an opening lined with aluminum provides passage between the dining and living rooms. Like an unforeseen intruder, a backlit picture of the Simpsons hangs amid studio self-portraits taken around the world—in Turkey, Japan, India, and Portugal.

LEFT: The bedroom follows a Chinese theme with its lacquered and gilt resin walls. Dragons flank the woven wicker headboard; garden lanterns are given a decorative oriental touch; and a synthetic tiger skin lies on the inlaid linoleum floor.

RIGHT: The kitchen has a mirrored ceiling; sparkling mosaics cover the walls. A tiled geometric design decorates the central island; on the backsplash are Turkish and Indian stickers featuring the faces of actors and singers. Doors made of mirrors and wood filigree conceal the storage cupboards.

BELOW, LEFT: In a corner of the dining room with a faux stone wall, pet dogs Lili and Toto assume a pose in front of their Ladybug and Bee abodes, which were brought back from a trip to Bangkok. The garden gnome appears to be in the middle of a body-building session.

BELOW, RIGHT: Tiles in earth and sun colors cover the entire kitchen—even the cabinet interiors.

ON THE ÎLE SAINT-LOUIS

With the Seine on one side and a garden on the other, Olivier Gagnère—a designer of furniture, decorative objects, and interiors—furnished his own apartment on the ground floor of a seventeenth-century *hôtel particulier*, or town house. He was charmed by the height of the ceilings, the scale of the rooms laid out in an enfilade, the abundant sunlight, and the sense of being in the country while living in the heart of Paris.

ABOVE: The dining room overlooks the garden. Since it faces north, this room is used for dinner, while lunch is served in the library. The walls are painted a deep charcoal gray, also used in the upholstery of Olivier's chairs; this color gives a lovely lighting effect in the evening, creating a tranquil atmosphere enlivened by a few touches of color. Cupboards are concealed behind the mirrored doors flanking the imitation wood mantelpiece.

ABOVE: The library receives ample sunlight, and Olivier Gagnère chose a deep Pompeian red that flatters the complexion. The same color also appears in the kilim carpets. The leopard chair, reminiscent of a tribal throne, was designed for the furniture gallery Neotu.

TOP, RIGHT: A pottery wine cooler from the Provençal town of Vallauris, crystal glasses designed by the master of the house, and Arts and Crafts lamps reissued by Florence Lopez are featured in the dining room. A table draped with Napoleon III Suzani embroidery is used for serving.

BOTTOM, RIGHT: A happy juxtaposition of shapes and materials: in the living room, a Syrian chest inlaid with mother-of-pearl stands next to a table displaying a group of silver-mounted shells, souvenirs from the East Indies.

ABOVE, LEFT: In the library, whose window overlooks a quay along the Seine, an elaborate pewter gilt Rajasthan chair stands near a Murano glass vase by Olivier Gagnère.

ABOVE, RIGHT: Traveler's trunks stand by invitingly in the vestibule, seemingly awaiting an imminent departure.

LEFT: Illuminated by two tall windows overlooking the Seine, the living room's stylish look is a tribute to the art of synthesis. Furnishings and decorative objects from Asia and the Middle East mingle with works by Olivier Gagnère; the embroidered fabrics shift from one table or sofa to another in a nomadic spirit, depending on the owner's whim.

FACING PAGE: Rooms follow one another in an enfilade in the Italian style, with the doorways located just behind the building's facade; the library can only be reached through the living room.

PARISIAN CHARM

MUCH-LOVED AND FEEL-GOOD HOMES

PAGE 182: A bouquet arranged in a vase; a dish piled high with fallen petals; and a table freshly polished with fragrant wax: simplicity is the essence of charm.

FACING PAGE, CLOCKWISE FROM TOP LEFT:
A collection of crystal vases and decorative objects is arranged on a console.

A gentleman's portrait, a plaster cast of a classical original, and a painting dating from the 1930s.

A table set with a flower-bedecked cloth, Chinese porcelain, antique silver, and pewter goblets.

The spirit of a country kitchen: copper pots and stoneware containers.

Hidden away in Paris are quiet, little-known byways, where apparently undistinguished facades conceal enchanting apartments. They seem to exist out of time, like an oasis of parkland amid the clamor of the city. The creak of an old staircase, the worn exposed beams of a former studio, the uneven glass of ancient windowpanes, and weathered oak floorboards extending into the kitchen all seem to remind us of familiar places filled with happy memories.

The pale pastels that cover these walls and floors have an undeniable appeal—soft shades of blue, lavender, pale green, and yellows so light as to be almost indiscernible. The wallpapers—whether original or reproductions—feature floral motifs in delicate little patterns suited to the interior of a country house. The modest furnishings blend discreetly into the subdued decor. Some articles are tributes to bygone artisanal skills—handcrafted pieces, polished on innumerable occasions, that have acquired the patina of time. Other pieces have been passed down from generation to generation: soft sofas piled with worn cushions, lamps bedecked with prisms, armoires whose paint is worn by the passage of time. Other furnishings might hail from a château or from a cinema, making their own contribution to our dreams and flights of fancy.

Cotton, linen, muslin, and lace—fabrics play an essential role with their faded hues. Silks are often richly embroidered, and the old velvets that cover the windows and seats are exquisitely light and soft. Treasured objects, new and old, mingle together unself-consciously, making their own statements. Some are found at a flea market or thrift store; others are bought during travels further afield. They respond to a very real yearning for memories of happy moments from the past, diffusing a certain sense of nostalgia that pervades rooms perfumed with flowers, whatever the season.

NEAR THE PORTE DE VERSAILLES

Véronique Lopez's home was built in 1860. Its windowless facade gives no hint of the charming interior, whose windows overlook a garden. Its quaint furnishings blend harmoniously with family treasures. Behind the discreet front door there lies an interior full of surprises.

LEFT: In a house that is frequently used for entertaining, the ground floor lends itself to a variety of theatrical settings. Here we see an evocation of a private luncheon in a 1900s hotel suite, arranged around a settee that Proust might have used.

FACING PAGE: The bedrooms are on the third floor, open to sunlight and overlooking the garden's grand trees. This bedroom is painted sunflower yellow, setting off the lines of a rustic eighteenth-century dressing table.

PAGES 188–89: There are two interconnecting living rooms on the main floor. The first, furnished with pieces from a family home and landscapes reminiscent of the Barbizon School, is a spot in which to chat, read, and play. The second, glimpsed through the doorway, is the place to enjoy an aperitif or coffee, seated by a fireplace crowned with a nineteenth-century mirror.

RIGHT: The staircase leading to the living room and bedrooms has a rustic simplicity with its cast-iron balustrades, flawlessly smooth banister, and simply polished oak steps.

BELOW: At one end of the main room on the ground floor, a monumental fireplace that would seem at home in a setting by Cocteau or Christian Bérard demarcates the kitchen area; the adjoining piece is the work of an artisan whose design was inspired by a butcher's block.

LEFT: The bed is enchanting and magical, its columns bedecked with a lacework of shells. It was made for the film *Un Amour de Sorcière* (*Witch's Way of Love*) starring Jeanne Moreau and Vanessa Paradis.

BELOW, LEFT: Three windows and two French doors illuminate the large room that opens onto the garden. For a sunlit luncheon, the table is set with a flowered cloth, pewter goblets, diamond-cut wineglasses, and a lighting fixture bedecked with hydrangeas.

BELOW, RIGHT: Giving the impression of a garden entrance, trellises run along the walls between the windows and French doors. Painted metal Portuguese wall fixtures cast a dramatic light in the evening, creating a theatrical ambience.

IN THE MARAIS

Fashion designer Vanessa Bruno has a home that seems far removed from the whirlwind of her latest collection and the stress of fashion shows. She surrounds herself with simple furnishings and little treasures, often discovered at flea markets. Soft pastel hues mingle with airy embroideries and floral fragrances.

LEFT: A few thoughtful details suffice to define the spirit of the living room: the graceful curves of a 1950s table, a bouquet of peonies, cups of frosted glass, and an Astronaut Snoopy added as an affectionate touch.

FACING PAGE: In the living room, which gives access to the bedroom, the rug is a square cut from a wall-to-wall carpet. Paper lanterns by Noguchi go from floor to ceiling in an interplay of form and material. The bed is glimpsed beyond the open door, the only touch of color in a subdued setting that is enlivened by a crystal chandelier sparkling like a precious jewel.

PAGES 194–95: All is calm, and an instinct for fashion is in evidence. Poplin covers the Napoleon III sofa; the curtains are cut from a voile used to make blouses; the silk covering the pillows is embroidered; and the artwork by Paola Levi is fashioned from glass beads.

FACING PAGE: Just before the living room lies a room reserved for watching television, or for guest accommodation. In the background, a shower is installed behind a glass enclosure.

RIGHT: A nineteenth-century mirror reflects a child's bedroom that is also accessible through the living room. The motifs of the carpet blend together in a pastel harmony.

BELOW, LEFT: In the corridor leading from the entry, above the Napoleon III chairs covered with pale pink velvet, a top from Vanessa Bruno's collection and some "trousseau treasures" are hung together pell-mell.

BELOW, RIGHT: A nineteenth-century embroidered silk shawl is thrown across the back of an armchair in Vanessa's bedroom; a "Lune" bag lies beside the armrest.

NEAR THE PONT DE L'ALMA

A few steps away from the Seine, Michelle Joubert—an interior designer who divides her time between Paris and Venice—has reimagined the conventions of a Haussmann-era building. She color-washed the walls in pale ocher, selected the furniture and accessories with no preconceived ideas, and took her time finding the right place for each of them.

ABOVE: A careful blend of genres and styles gives the living room a timeless appeal. The room's large scale accommodates an imposing vitrine arranged to suggest a cabinet of curiosities, capacious Italian and English armchairs, a sculptor's modeling base deployed as a coffee table, a monumental head, and a giant clam shell. In the background, the curtain in a small adjacent room can be glimpsed.

BELOW: On the walls of the entrance hall, two nineteenth-century mirrors, still in their original frames, are hung opposite each other, creating the illusion of infinite depth.

TOP, RIGHT: The entrance hall also serves as a dining room. A window with small panes of glass mounted in lead and doors with moldings painted in brown are reminiscent of a Dutch interior, a style that was not uncommon in nineteenth-century Parisian apartments.

BOTTOM, RIGHT: In the living room, facing the vitrine in a flawlessly symmetrical arrangement, the mirror's frame and *trumeau* are painted a subtle off-white that elegantly complements the gray mantelpiece.

FACING PAGE: The kitchen has been modernized from top to bottom, with matte black paint that contrasts with the gleaming tile backsplash.

BELOW: In the living room's vitrine, the mistress of the house has placed a painting of Venice, her second favorite city after Paris.

TOP, RIGHT: Michelle Joubert's home will always include a stuffed and mounted animal, traveling mementoes, eccentric articles such as this trompe l'oeil chair, and the slightly faded colors that she regards as indestructible.

BOTTOM, RIGHT: The bedroom window with its silk curtains overlooks the most Parisian of vistas: a view of the Eiffel Tower that sparkles across the Seine once evening falls. The sight can be enjoyed reclining on the bed or seated in the theater armchair.

RUE DES PLANTES

Fashion designer Loulou de la Falaise succumbed to the charms of the light and space offered by an artist's studio. The apartment consists of an expansive area with a mezzanine. It shows her distinctive touch and Bohemian flair. Her own discoveries—like precious jewels—blend with gifts from her friends.

LEFT: A Louis XVI bed—which Maxime de la Falaise, Loulou's mother, had in her New York apartment—stands by a column from a secondhand shop, a terra-cotta cachepot, and a simple folding table. All are arranged in a skillful composition of colors and styles that reveals the talents of this woman of fashion.

FACING PAGE: "I'm in the clouds," Loulou de la Falaise said when she first entered the room, and this impression of airiness and lightness has never left her. She has furnished this perfectly cubic space, with its eighteen-foot-high (6 m) ceiling, with the things she loves best: theater furniture, family memorabilia, and other objects that have stories to tell.

RIGHT: On a low wall at the foot of the staircase leading to the mezzanine, a mirror reflects an array of carefully selected objects: a bronze bust of her father Alain de la Falaise; cherubs mounted on an eighteenth-century candelabrum, and a painting by her friend Béatrice Caracciolo.

BELOW: In the library beneath the mezzanine, two mirrors face each other: one is nineteenth century and framed in gilt wood; the other, a work by Gaudí in mahogany, was a gift from Ricardo Bofill. Chairs from Maison de Couture surround the table; they were formerly in the salons of Kenzo and Yves Saint Laurent.

LEFT: Loulou wanted a spectacular interior, from top to bottom. A nine-foot (3 m) chandelier, salvaged from Claridge's hotel, sets the tone. It was restored and remounted by a flea-market dealer who had just purchased a batch of crystal prisms in Bohemia. Equally theatrical, the mirror framed in gilt wood formerly belonged to Samuel Bernard, Louis XIV's banker; it dominates the room, its height rivaling the latticework columns loaned by a friend and subsequently forgotten.

BELOW, LEFT: Simple white cotton curtains are hung in the mezzanine bedroom; a Moroccan mirror found in Marrakech and armchairs draped with Indian cottons are souvenirs of travels and visits to artisans' workshops.

BELOW, RIGHT: Arranged in front of a Japanese painting, glasses, porcelains, opaline vessels, an art-deco flask, vases in the Japanese style with floral decoration, and a charming art-nouveau piece attest to a sure eye and a taste for fine things.

IN BOULOGNE-BILLANCOURT

It took a year of work for interior designer Julie Isoré to convert a laboratory into a family home, while preserving the original structure. None of the rooms is on the same level. They are connected by a labyrinth of staircases, illuminated by a glass wall that opens out onto the terrace.

LEFT: Magnetic paint on the kitchen walls allows drawings and reminders to be posted with simple magnets. Deep black paint and a gunmetal chair set the tone. Everything is simplified, and nothing is fragile.

FACING PAGE: The kitchen is a former atelier featuring a glass wall with metal mountings. Behind the open door at the end of the corridor, a few steps lead to a split level, where the living and dining rooms are combined in a single space, with an eighteen-foot-high (6 m) ceiling, that runs the length of the terrace.

FACING PAGE: The uncluttered living room is reminiscent of a loft. Office furnishings combine with Scandinavian design, striving for an essential simplicity that complements evocative objects, often random finds. Knoll stools, designed by Saarinen, are placed in front of a large, zinc letter "D," propped up like a painting.

BELOW: An eighteen-foot-high (6 m) ceiling allowed the installation of a mezzanine, which is reached by a staircase leading up from the living room.

TOP, RIGHT: The master bedroom and the bathroom are situated on the mezzanine, creating a duplex.

BOTTOM, RIGHT: Tom Dixon's fixtures provide lighting for the dining room, which is furnished with a farmhouse table and a half-stripped country cupboard. The dining and living rooms share a living space that opens onto the terrace.

ON LE SENTIER

In collaboration with decorator Michel Pinet, Philippe Irrmann converted a simple space—which was once lit by a red-light district's neon glare—into a very traditional gentleman's abode. The authenticity of its decor conveys the tastes and customs of the late eighteenth and early nineteenth centuries.

ABOVE: The color of the walls and moldings in the vestibule has been chosen based on period archives. Decorative motifs have been painted on the door leading to the small sitting room by a specialized restorer of historic monuments, inspired by the same source. If Philippe Irrmann needs to use a computer, he sets it up on an eighteenth-century backgammon table and uses an oil lamp for illumination!

BELOW: The table is set with graceful eighteenth-century wineglasses and a faience soup tureen made in the Manufacture de Pont-aux-Choux, a Parisian manufactory created in 1743.

TOP, RIGHT: In an apartment illuminated by candlelight, the dining-room table is set in the vestibule with eighteenth-century china: Sèvres porcelain plates, a "Pont-aux-Choux" soup tureen, and Louis XV candelabra.

BOTTOM, RIGHT: The living-room walls are covered with wallpaper reproduced from late eighteenth-century designs. The decorative objects, paintings, engravings, and armillary spheres all evoke the "Grand Tour," undertaken by young gentlemen in the eighteenth century to explore other civilizations and cultures.

RIGHT: In the pantry, all necessary kitchen equipment is hidden away in storage cabinets to preserve the unity of the decor. Only the cast-iron stove is visible.

BELOW, LEFT: In this kitchen in the heart of Paris, meals are cooked over a wood fire in a ceiling-high hearth, just as they would have been in the eighteenth century. The opening for the "*potagers*" can be glimpsed to the left. It was filled with hot embers to cook dishes requiring gentle heat.

BELOW, RIGHT: The elegant monogrammed napkins testify to the history of these fine linens, which were patiently embroidered by nuns in their convent workshops.

LEFT: Wallpaper—a carefully researched reproduction based on an eighteenth-century design—covers the bedroom walls. History suggests that the initials embroidered in gold thread in the gilt frame are those of Queen Marie-Antoinette.

BELOW, LEFT: In the bedroom, the Empire bed is set in an alcove hung with iridescent silk taffeta. One door opens into the bathroom, and another is hidden beneath a hanging, as in centuries gone by.

BELOW, RIGHT: In a classic enfilade, the antechamber and the bedroom offer a quintessential eighteenth-century vista.

ACKNOWLEDGMENTS

It is never easy to allow a photographer to intrude into one's home. It involves revealing far more than just one's living space. Furnished with loving care, often over a period of years, each of these Parisian residences reflects its owner's most secret and intimate self. I offer my sincere thanks to each and every person who opened up their homes for their generosity and cordial reception.

A number of these articles were written with the amicable and talented cooperation of Anne Rogier, published in the magazine *Point de Vue*, and she is equally deserving of our thanks. I also wish to express my gratitude to other companions on this voyage of discovery—without them, this book would not have been the same: Diane Cazelles, for our explorations of the environs of Paris (*Made in Banlieues*, Éditions de La Martinière); Philippe Seulliet, who is always eager to share his discovery of remarkable locations; Marie Bariller, who keeps a watchful eye on fashion and designers (*Espaces privés*, Éditions Aubanel); Anne Swynghedauw, who helped me to explore the world of Sarah Lavoine (Éditions de La Martinière); and Catherine Synave, a journalist who has specialized in reporting on the decorative arts for many years, and who provided exactly the right terms to describe each of these stylistic adventures. Finally, for bringing the editorial project to fruition and ensuring it reflects all the aspirations and pleasures of these encounters, I give an appreciative salute to the enthusiasm and attentiveness of the talented team at Flammarion—Ghislaine Bavoillot, Boris Guilbert, and Isabelle Ducat.

Guillaume de Laubier

Special thanks to Guillaume de Laubier, who suggested that I embark on this adventure; to Ghislaine Bavoillot, who had such confidence in me; and to Boris Guilbert for his patient guidance. Thank you also to all those who spoke with me so informatively and eloquently about their homes, making an invaluable contribution to the preparation of the text and captions.

Catherine Synave

Editorial Director: Ghislaine Bavoillot
Design: Isabelle Ducat
Translated from the French by Elizabeth Heard
Copyediting: Penelope Isaac
Typesetting: Gravemaker+Scott
Proofreading: Davina Thackara
Color Separation: IGS-CP, L'Isle d'Espagnac, France
Printed in Slovenia by Gorenjski tisk

Simultaneously published in French as *Maison parisienne*
© Flammarion, S.A., Paris, 2014

English-language edition
© Flammarion, S.A., Paris, 2014

FACING PAGE: In a living room, nineteenth-century vases decorated with classical motifs and mounted as lamp bases are juxtaposed with pictorial works that are characteristic of twentieth-century art.

PAGE 216: The carpeting of a Parisian loft's mezzanine features geometric motifs, complementing a 1951 armchair signed by Marco Zanuso.